T0065788

50 YEARS OF LIVING, LEARNING, LOVING & LAUGHING

SABRINA REEVES PARTEE

WESTBOW
PRESS®
A DIVISION OF THOMAS NELSON
& ZONDERVAN

Copyright © 2022 Sabrina Reeves Partee.

All rights reserved. No part of this book may be used or reproduced by any means, graphic, electronic, or mechanical, including photocopying, recording, taping or by any information storage retrieval system without the written permission of the author except in the case of brief quotations embodied in critical articles and reviews.

WestBow Press books may be ordered through booksellers or by contacting:

WestBow Press
A Division of Thomas Nelson & Zondervan
1663 Liberty Drive
Bloomington, IN 47403
www.westbowpress.com
844-714-3454

Because of the dynamic nature of the Internet, any web addresses or links contained in this book may have changed since publication and may no longer be valid. The views expressed in this work are solely those of the author and do not necessarily reflect the views of the publisher, and the publisher hereby disclaims any responsibility for them.

Any people depicted in stock imagery provided by Getty Images are models, and such images are being used for illustrative purposes only. Certain stock imagery © Getty Images.

ISBN: 978-1-6642-8428-9 (sc)
ISBN: 978-1-6642-8429-6 (hc)
ISBN: 978-1-6642-8427-2 (e)

Library of Congress Control Number: 2022921580

Print information available on the last page.

WestBow Press rev. date: 11/16/2022

This book is dedicated to the memory of my father, Elder Reginald Charles Reeves; my aunt, Mildred Derricks; and my sister friend, Christina "Nina" Smith.

CONTENTS

Game of Life

Reflections

FOREWORD

Growing up isn't easy. Mindsets may change. The ways we view self and others shift, and with that comes the metamorphosis of identity. In her book, *50 Years of Living, Learning, Loving, and Laughing,* Sabrina Reeves Partee invites us to reflect on and pinpoint our quests for belonging. Through topics of nostalgia, friendship, purpose, and spirituality, we are beckoned to journal our own voices. These thought-provoking subjects help us to connect our feelings and experiences as we search our souls for our truths.

In order to feel secure in our decisions, we may need to take a step back to see the big picture. This book allows us to stop, take a deep breath, and think before we proceed. Self-actualization and self-introspection are the goals of this book. Growth comes when we discover our inner courage to take the steps necessary to achieve positive change. And *50 Years of Living, Learning, Loving, and Laughing* brings us to where we are able to make mature decisions that produce results. Through its pages, we get a better understanding of who we really are at the core of our human experiences. A better grasp of our realities empowers us to think our way through the ebbs and flows of life.

We are the masters of our destinies, but first we may need to face our giants through self-scrutiny. Analyzing our decisions at life's crossroads may require us to dig deep and look for answers. As we utilize the journal entries to help us translate our feelings into clear thoughts on paper, we are evolving into our best selves.

Dr. Judith Williams,
Fellow Truth Seeker

PREFACE

I began writing my thoughts down at a young age. Every night before I prayed and went to bed, I would write about my day in my diary. In my twenties, my diary matured into a journal, and now it is a combination of both diary and journal (diarjournal). During my teenage years, I started writing down quotes and poems. I often share quotes and poems with others when I want to encourage, motivate, or convey a particular message. Throughout the years, I have penned quotes and poems in my diarjournal.

In September 2012, I published some of the poems from my diarjournal and shared them with my family and friends. I was encouraged by the response I received and inspired to write more poems. In 2015, I published my first book of poetry, *Words of Wisdom for Women*. I was overwhelmed by the feedback from readers. So in 2020, I published *My Time on Earth*, a journal of poetry and quotes. I asked readers of both books to let me know which poems they liked the most. Readers, thank you for your feedback! You helped me determine which quotes and poems to include in *50 Years of Living, Learning, Loving, and Laughing*.

Since publishing my last book, I've been asked where can copies of the first book be purchased. Unfortunately, the publisher that published my first book is no longer in business. Instead of simply republishing my first book, I decided to write a third book. *50 Years of Living, Learning, Loving, and Laughing* includes fourteen poems from my first book, eleven new poems, and fourteen new quotes.

While reading, I encourage readers to ask themselves these three questions: What are my thoughts after reading this poem or quote? Is this something I have experienced? How can I help others experiencing this? I also hope readers take the time to reflect and respond to the reflection questions in the space provided.

WHAT READERS ARE SAYING

The quotes and poems were very inspiring. My favorite poems are "Game of Life" and "Staying Sane." They gave me a lot to think about and focus on. After I finish high school, I am thinking about writing. I do not know what kind of writer I want to be, but I am inspired by Sabrina.

—Serenity

I would encourage you to read, *50 Years of Living, Learning, Loving, and Laughing.* I read *Words of Wisdom for Women.* The most engaging feature of the poems is how they explore the reality of human life. Each poem is a showpiece on its own.

—Christy Johnson

I truly enjoyed reading the quotes and poems from this book. They are truly thought-provoking, inspirational, and help me to see life from a different perspective. A lot of the quotes and poems made me reflect on things that I have experienced in my everyday dealings with family, friends, and just life struggles in general. They help me see how I dealt with or overcame certain things that took place at that time of my life. This book also allowed me to see how I can look at things that come up in life differently going forward. These poems and quotes cover all aspects of life, ranging from humorous subjects to loss and pain that we may face as we deal with life's uncertainties. I encourage others to buy this book and others that are by Sabrina Reeves Partee if you are looking for inspiration on how to have the right attitude when dealing with this thing called life!

—Zettica Mitchell

5 Star. Very inspirational/encouraging poems and quotes. I lost my cousin/sister last year (2021), and I was in a very dark place. I went into depression and felt like there was no hope. I felt like I would never see the light again until I opened *My Time on Earth,* poetry-quote journal. God led me to the poem "Depression." This poem was on time for me and blessed me tremendously. It even brought the light back into my life. I wanted this book to bless others just as it blessed me, so I purchased over ten copies and blessed my coworkers. They absolutely love it! It's a book you can always refer to when you need to be encouraged. Sabrina Reeves Partee wrote this book from her heart, and it shows. Very well written, and I'm looking forward to reading her third book, *50 Years of Living, Learning, Loving, and Laughing.*

—Jessica Wilkerson

As I reread the quotes, my heart began to flutter as if I had read them for the first time. "Learn How to Say No and Don't Feel Bad about It" reminded me that my no is okay, and I do not need to explain it. The second one that hit me like a ton of bricks reads, "What if the past three years, were the last three years of your life? Would you have done anything differently." Within moments, I felt joy and sadness. Joy because I accomplished a few things, and sadness because I haven't accomplished the majority of what my heart desires. Sabrina is a very passionate writer. I find her quotes to be thought-provoking, deep, uplifting, encouraging, and inspiring. She writes with the pencil of her heart.

The poem "Pictures" took me back to when my children were babies. As times passes, I forget what they were like until I look at pictures. When I look at their pictures, I feel the exact emotions I felt during the time the pictures were taken and feel as though I am back in the moment. Sabrina is a phenomenal writer who has the ability to touch one's mind and soul with her words. I purchased six copies of *My Time on Earth* for the women's group, and each of them expressed how much they enjoyed reading them.

—Kenya M. Hampton

QUOTES TO LIVE BY

QUOTES FOR JANUARY

A new year feels like you've just been
baptized in the Pacific Ocean.

Everything you need to know about life can be learned by reading the book of Genesis.

What if the past three years were the last three years of your life?
Would you have done anything differently?

QUOTES FOR FEBRUARY

Surviving a life-changing surgery or illness gives you a new lease on life and time to rent your body a little while longer.

I'm going to keep on being me; that's the only person I know how to be. No matter what others say, I'm going to keep on being this way.

Marry someone who will encourage you to become closer to God, not further away from Him.

QUOTES FOR MARCH

Train your body to be healthy in your youth, and when you are old, it will not shut down on you.

This is the advice I would give my eighteen-year-old self: To be successful in life, you have to plan. But remember, your life will not turn out like you planned it.

Encouragement and an education help you have successful endeavors.

QUESTIONS FOR THE FIRST QUARTER

1. What are some things you can do differently this year?
2. How can you improve your health?
3. What advice would you give an eighteen-year-old?

QUOTES FOR APRIL

When you ask for help and don't get it, ask again
and again until you get the help you want.

Don't waste your time and upset yourself trying to explain your daily struggles to people you know will not understand. This will only make you more frustrated.

The effect of continuously processing the passing of people you know very well is like sitting in a doctor's office waiting for Dr. Death to call your name.

QUOTES FOR MAY

When it comes to people, don't have favorites because
you may not be your favorite person's favorite.

Give people what they need, not what you think they need.

Our grandparents are the original roof of our family house,
supporting the family through life's storms. When our grandparents
are no longer on the earth, our parents and their siblings become
the new roof. The grandchildren's job is to make sure there are no
holes in the new roof, so the family house remains protected from
family storms.

QUOTES FOR JUNE

Do not argue with a person if you know the argument will
not change his or her mind or opinion about a topic.

Be quiet! Breathe! Pray! Think! Talk!

Cherish the little stuff! It's the little stuff—cards, calls, conversations—you'll miss the most when loved ones are gone. The little stuff that only they did for you. Always cherish the little stuff.

QUESTIONS FOR THE SECOND QUARTER

1. What would you like more help with?
2. What do you need from others but aren't getting?
3. What are some little things you can do for others?

QUOTES FOR JULY

No matter what you say or how you say it, someone
will be offended. Always be yourself, and don't worry
about what others think or say about you.

It does not matter how wise you are, you will become even wiser
if you listen to the opinions of others.

When you depart the earth, your treasures sometimes become someone else's trash. Give your treasures to those you treasure before you depart.

QUOTES FOR AUGUST

If you want to truly understand someone, start
with learning about her or his childhood.

Parents ought not to be depressed or frustrated when their children fail to meet their expectations. Parents, perhaps you didn't meet your parents' expectations either.

Respect people's thoughts, ideas, and property. Respect people with authority over you and those older than you. Respect them even if they don't respect you.

QUOTES FOR SEPTEMBER

A friend is someone you can trust not to tell your darkest secrets even after you have told all his or hers.

If you have no expectations of people, you don't get your feelings hurt.

Don't tell people, "I've been thinking about you." Show them you've been thinking about them.

QUESTIONS FOR THE THIRD QUARTER

1. What are some things you treasure?
2. What do you wish others knew about your childhood?
3. How can you be a better friend this year?

QUOTES FOR OCTOBER

Hope is to life what air is to the lungs.

Learn how to say no and not feel bad about it!

I try to compete with myself, not others. I don't have the same skills, talents, or opportunities they have, so it would be an unfair competition.

QUOTES FOR NOVEMBER

Each person should have a cause she or he is passionate about. If you help me with my cause, and I help you with your cause, the world will be a much better place for all of us.

Pick up the pieces of life and move forward.

Be careful how you treat others because you don't know how or when you might see them again.

QUOTES FOR DECEMBER

We often search online to find out more about others. Sometimes we need to google our names to see what information comes up about us.

When it comes to our futures, all we can do is pray and plan. God will prepare us for it.

If you died today, what would others say about you?

QUESTIONS FOR THE FOURTH QUARTER

1. What are some of your skills and talents?
2. What are you hopeful about?
3. What cause can you support next year?

OBSERVATIONS

BOOKS

Fiction,
Nonfiction.

Novel,
Short Story.

Biography,
Autobiography.

Hardback,
Paperback.

Books take you places you may never visit,
Introduce you to people you may never meet.

Books can be friends when you're lonely
And heal a broken heart.

Books let you experience an event you did not attend.
Allow you to relive the past and imagine the future.

Books outlive us all.
They were here before we came
And will remain long after we are gone.

TELEVISION

News,
Weather.

Entertainment,
Education.

Cooking,
Shopping.

Comedy,
Drama.

Reality,
Documentary.

Talk show,
Design show.

Are you looking for a new school, church, job, or family?
Watch TV.

Do you want to buy a car?
Watch TV.

Do you want to learn how to cook?
Watch TV.

Need ideas for your new home?
Watch TV.

Need child-rearing advice?
Watch TV.

Everything you need for life is on TV.
So watch TV.

MAIL

Email,
Snail mail,
Junk mail.

I like sending mail.
I like receiving mail.
I like reading my mail.

Our mail reflects who we are
And who we are trying to be.
It is like a diary open for everyone to read.

It reveals where we shop,
Our interests and hobbies,
Who we owe,
Our friends,
Political affiliations,
Religious beliefs.
Our past and present,
Our future plans.

Mail is private and public at the same time.
We know who sent it, but until we open it,
We don't know what's in it.
Mail.

FOOD

Food—

You can live with it,
But you won't survive long without it.
So why not enjoy it?

One commercial says eat this.
Another advertisement says don't eat that.
Food—
Why not enjoy it?

That drink makes you sick.
This vitamin makes you well.
Food—
Why not enjoy it?

One research study indicates this.
Another study says that
You must eat this;
You can't eat that.
Food—
Just enjoy it!

PICTURES

Pictures capture moments in our lives,
Everyday life and special occasions.
We can learn a lot by looking at pictures.
Pictures remind us of the fashions and fads of days gone by.
Who attended an event, and who did not.
They show where we like to go and what we like to do.
If we put them all together, they tell a story.
Our story.
Our family's story.
A story about our life and times.

FAMILY

Mothers,
Fathers.

Sisters,
Brothers.

Daughters,
Sons.

Grandmothers,
Grandfathers.

Aunts,
Uncles.

Nieces,
Nephews.

Cousins,
Friends.

They are all family.

We share a connection that we cannot fully explain.
We share experiences that outsiders don't understand.
Our entire lives are in some way shaped by family.

It makes no difference if you are a member by birth or choice,
You are loved the same.
My little cousin once said, "Family is a beautiful thing."

PREACHERS

Preachers are people.
Preachers are people too.
Just like me and you.
They need for us to

Love them,
Show concern for them,
Support them,
To try to understand them,
Forgive them when needed,
Be patient with them,
And most important, pray for them.

COWORKERS

Coworkers—
Allies,
Enemies,
In between.

Coworkers—
By chance, you'll meet one that who becomes a true friend.

Coworkers—
Some years you spend more time with them than with your family.

Coworkers—
They know the real you.
The you, you can hide from others.

Coworkers.

DRIVING TO WORK

Running late again.
Almost involved in
A road rage incident.
Never-ending construction,
Lanes blocked off.
Slow cars,
Stalled cars,
Accidents,
Red lights.

Finished getting ready in the car.
Combed my hair,
Put on my masks and gloves.
Listened to music on Sirius XM.
Thought about today's to-do list.
Whew! I finally made it to work!
Going to run inside and report for morning duty.

OBSERVATIONS CHECKPOINT

1. What are some of your favorite books?
2. What does your mail say about you?
3. How would you describe your family?

GAME OF LIFE

GAME OF LIFE

At birth, you're in.
When you die, you're out.

Earth is the game board.
All humans are players.

Spin the spinner to see what you get—
Good health,
Long life,
Fancy cars,
Multiple houses,
Successful career,
Plenty of money.

Losing a turn means—
Job loss,
Losing someone you love,
Dashed hopes,
Deferred dreams.

When you're born, you're in.
Will you win or lose?

DEPRESSION

Depression makes you want to scream.
Depression messes with your dreams.
It makes you too tired to do anything.
Depression is no plaything.

Coming out of depression is easier said than done.
Start by doing something fun.
Go outside, and get energy from the sun.
Sing a little song.
Stop stressing about what is wrong.
Be thankful for what you have.
Remember you still have time to get things done.

If you do these things every day,
Little by little,
Your depression will fade away.

SETBACKS

When you have a setback,
Fall down, and then get back up.
Reflect,
Regroup,
Recharge.
Learn from your mistakes.

Figure out what you did wrong and try again.
Realize your setback is a learning experience
That one day, you can share with someone else to help him or her
through a setback.
Remember: God's timing is perfect, even in a setback.

SLOW DOWN

Slow down.
Soak in the sunshine
While reading a book.
Then call a friend.

Slow down.
Take a siesta,
Exercise,
Solve a puzzle.

Slow down.
Visit someone,
Take a relaxing bath,
Eat your favorite snack,
Daydream.
Slow down.

MISCARRIAGE

My miscarriage.
No one wants to talk about it but me.
It seems as if it forever affected my psyche.
I can't shake it off and be free.
Was it something I did that caused it to be?
I can't figure out why it happened to my body?

My miscarriage.
Was the baby a girl or boy?
Supposedly miscarriages occur frequently.
Was this my only chance at pregnancy?
No one told me how mentally hard it would be.
Was something wrong with the baby, or was it just me?

My miscarriage.
I guess the full-term pregnancy was not to be.
Would the baby and I have died during delivery?
I never expected this, you see.
Why did this have to happen to my first baby?
Why did it have to be?

LET IT GO

Let it go!
Let it go!
Let it go!

Cry!
Laugh!
Pray!

Do whatever you need to do to let it go.
Throw a shoe against the wall.
Scream as you run down the hall.

Write a letter.
Call a friend.
It will make you sick if you keep it in.

Get it all out!
Let it go!
Let it go!

DIVORCE

Someone told me, "A divorce is like a living death."
I say, "That is a fact."
Divorce is also
Traumatic,
Life-altering,
Chaotic.

And it leaves you feeling
Rejected,
Abandoned,
Angry.
Divorce is like a wound that heals on the outside
But never heals on the inside.

MOVING OUT

I'm moving out!
I've been here far too long, and it's past time to move on.
I've overstayed my welcome,
So it's time to "hit the door"!

I see my boxes strewn across the floor.
Piles everywhere—
A pile for the trash,
Another pile to take,
And a pile for things to donate.

I can hear the hum of the moving truck,
Arriving to take my personal belongings to my new location.
I feel like a baby bird just learning how to fly.
After I finally settle in, I smell the scent of my new place.
I finally moved out!
Hooray!

STAYING SANE

Pedestrians darting in front of cars.
Drivers talking on the phone and running red lights.
The speed limit is 40, but the car in front of me is going 20 in the
fast lane.
I'm trying to stay sane in an insane world.

I finally make it to the store,
But I can't seem to pick the right lane.
Have to wait in line twenty minutes just to pay for one item.
Just trying to stay sane in an insane world.

Made it back home; I sit down and turn on the TV,
Watch the news, and what do I see?
Breaking news about someone killing eight members of their family.
People criticizing, complaining, arguing, yelling.
Trying to stay sane in an insane world.

Blizzards in the North.
Flooding in the South.
Hurricanes on the East Coast.
Earthquakes on the West Coast.
Tornados and wildfires in the state of Texas.
A war raging in Ukraine.
All of this is happening on the same day.
I'm trying to stay sane in an insane world.

GAME OF LIFE CHECKPOINTS

1. What are some setbacks you've had?
2. What do you need to let go?
3. How can you slow down?

REFLECTIONS

THE NEW YEAR

Every year in January I'm excited about the new year!
I have all 12 months ahead of me—
Jan, Feb, March,
April, May, June,
July, August, September,
October, November, December.

I wish I knew what will happen this year.
What will be the breaking news of the day?
What exciting things will happen?
Who will be born
And who will die?
What new things will be discovered?
What disaster will unfold?

I wish I knew what will happen this year that will change my life
forever.
Will I meet someone new who will remain in my life forever?
Will I make a decision that brings me closer to my lifelong dreams?
I wonder what this new year will bring.

BIRTHDAYS ARE FOR REFLECTING

Your birthday is the day you celebrate you!
It is also a time for reflection and introspection, but not depression.
Are you the same person you were ten years ago?
Have you changed for the better?
Think about what you want your life to be like ten years from now, and start making plans today!
Hope you have a happy birthday!

HAPPY

What makes me happy?
Eating chocolate candy.
Hearing my favorite song on the car radio.
Relaxing and watching TV.
Reading an enlightening book.
Observing a child finally learning something new.
Seeing the smile on someone's face after opening a surprise package.
Making others happy.
That's what makes me happy.

EXCUSES

I'm sick of excuses.
I know you are too.
Let me start by listing a few.
I got fired.
I already tried.
My daddy left my momma.

I don't have time to deal with all the drama.
If I hear another excuse,
I don't know what I might do.

I should probably make a sign that reads:
"Write all your excuses down.
Tear them up.
Put them in a machine.
Watch them spin around."

Why don't you follow my lead,
And do the same
If you are sick of playing
The Excuses Game?

MISUNDERSTOOD

All my life I've felt misunderstood.
I've been told,
"You're mean."
"You're too sensitive."
"You're spoiled."
"You're stubborn."
"You're too impatient."

But if you took the time to get to know me,
You would learn I'm
Trustworthy,
Honest,
Generous,
Considerate,
Sweet.
And yes, I'm sensitive
And stubborn too.
Now, what are some words that describe you?

LISTEN

Do you listen when she talks?
Do you see the way she walks?
Is she walking straight and tall?
Or is she slouched, like she might fall?

Listen!

Does he cry himself to sleep at night?
Is he afraid when you turn off the light?

Listen!

Was she saying, "Please help me,"
When she "accidentally" ran her car into a tree.

Listen!

What was he trying to say
When he suddenly lost a ton of weight."
Did you ask him was he okay?
Or did you say, "You look great!"

Listen!

Did you ask her about her day
Before you said, "Go away!"

Listen!

People are talking every day.
We need to listen to what they are trying to say.
Everyone needs a friend along the way.
So please listen!

ARE YOU A FRIEND?

Think about yourself.
Are you loyal and thoughtful?
Are you loving and caring?
Are you a giver or a taker?
Are you real or a faker?

A friend is
Available when you need her,
Unselfish with his time,
The first person you call when you have something to tell.

A friend
Spends more time listening than giving advice.
Can feel when things are not quite right.
Remembers your birthday, anniversaries, deaths, and significant events.

Go ahead and ask yourself,
"Am I a true friend?
Will I really be there until the end?"

IF ONLY I KNEW

If only I knew you would become terminally ill,
I would have told you, "Enjoy your good health while you have it."
If only I knew you would not live to see your graduation day,
I would have congratulated you on every accomplishment along the
way.

If only I knew you would not live to see forty,
I would have told you to live each day like it was your last.
If only I knew that would be the last text you would send me,
I would have saved it instead of deleting it.

If only I knew that was the last time you would call me,
I would have rushed to the phone instead of thinking, *I'll call back
later.*
If only I knew that was the last time I would hear your voice,
I would have committed it to memory.

If only I knew that was the last time I was going to see your face,
I would have taken your picture.
If only I knew that was our last argument,
I wouldn't have said, "I wish you were dead!"

If only I knew.
If only I knew.
I would have said, "I love you!"

LAST DAY

What would you do if you knew it was your last day?
What would you eat?
What would you wear?
How would you prepare to live your last day?
Your last day not by choice but by force.

Would you try to soak in every single minute?
Would you stay in bed all day?
Would you go outside and have some fun in the sun?
Or would you get on your knees and pray?

Would you call the people you loved and to say goodbye?
Or would you leave them a goodbye note.
Would you write down instructions on how you want to be remembered?
Or leave a video sharing your favorite memories.

You wouldn't have enough time to do all the things you planned to do.
It would be too late for people to form a different opinion about you.
Have you ever thought about what you would do on your last day?
Your last day not by choice but by force!

REFLECTIONS CHECKPOINT

1. What makes you happy?
2. What would you like to say to someone before it's too late?
3. Where do you see yourself in ten years?

040900072-00836378

Printed in the United States
by Baker & Taylor Publisher Services